Table of Contents

.... 1

Introduction 3

Twice Fried Extra Crispy Garlicky Russet Potatoes 4

Easy Kangaroo Stroganoff 6

Spicy Beer Battered Barramundi 8

Spicy Grilled Figs with Vanilla Ice cream 10

Sweet and Tangy Pavlova 12

Minty Flavor Roasted Baliman Bug 14

Double Chocolate Milo Pops 16

Spicy Grilled Kangaroo Meat in Tacos 18

Peanut Crusted Chicken Schnitzel 20

Aussie Pine Cap Burger Patties 22

Aussie Spicy Apricot Chicken 24

A little Mediterranean Twist on the Aussie Scone 26

Cinnamon-Chili Rub Pan-Fried Lamb Pops 28

Savory Impossible Pie 30

Chocolate and Nuts Cookies 32

Good Old Cornish Handheld Pastry 34

Beef Shashliks with Veggie on a stick 36

Minty, Spicy Lamb Pie 38

Pan-Fried Prawns with Chili Lime Cilantro Butter 40

Oven Fried Lemongrass Fish Wedges 42

Madura Green Tea Bag Fruit Loaf 44

Grilled Peaches and Feta Salad 46

Rich Caramel Filled Anzac Muffins 48

Vegemite Beef Roll 50

It is a Tim Tam Cheesecake 52

Lord Lamington's Lamingtons 54

As Easy As a Damper Loaf 56

Aussie Classic Chiko Rolls 58

Fresh and Down To Earth Salad 60

Sweet Mango and Chili Fried Prawns 62

Conclusion 64

Classic Australian Recipes that will Make You Visit

Classic Aussie Recipes that will Take You on a Journey

BY: Ida Smith

License Notes

This book is licensed for your personal enjoyment only. This book may not be re-sold or given away to other people. If you would like to share this book with another person, please purchase an additional copy for each recipient. If you're reading this book and did not purchase it, or it was not purchased for your use only, then please return to your favorite ebook retailer and purchase your own copy. Thank you for respecting the hard work of this author.

Introduction

Australia is the land of plenty. In what seems like a vast space of wasteland lies unique and incredible creatures that bring s a different taste to your taste buds. We have gone down under to get 30 classic dishes, and we only hope we can do justice to them.

If you are ready, so are we.

Twice Fried Extra Crispy Garlicky Russet Potatoes

These are delicious and the best way to eat potatoes.

Preparation Time: 60 minutes

Yield: 4

Ingredient List:

- 1 dozen medium-sized russet potatoes peeled
- 1 head garlic
- 1 L duck fat
- 1 sprig rosemary
- Salt and pepper

Preparation:
Add the potatoes with the garlic and rosemary in the oil

Add it to cook until a knife can pass through with some resistance
Remove and bring the oil to a high temperature (remove the garlic and rosemary too)
Return the potatoes to the hot oil to cook and crisp up
Sprinkle with salt and pepper before serving

Easy Kangaroo Stroganoff

Kangaroo is a native Australian wild species that apparently makes a good meal. It cooks low and slow to develop a rich and dark flavor with every bite.

Preparation Time: 150 minutes

Yield: 4

Ingredient List:

- 2 pounds kangaroo steak cut in large chunks
- 2 tbsp dark tomato paste
- 1 tbsp ketchup
- 500ml Massel chicken stock
- 2 tbsp oil
- 1 cup cornstarch
- 1 large onion chopped

- 200g portabella mushrooms sliced
- 1 tsp diced garlic
- 1 small chili chopped
- Salt and pepper
- Sour cream to serve

Preparation:
Add the oil to a slow cooker
Dust the kangaroo in flour and brown on all sides
Add the remaining ingredients except for the sour cream
Cover to cook low and slow until the meat is tender
Season to taste and serve

Spicy Beer Battered Barramundi

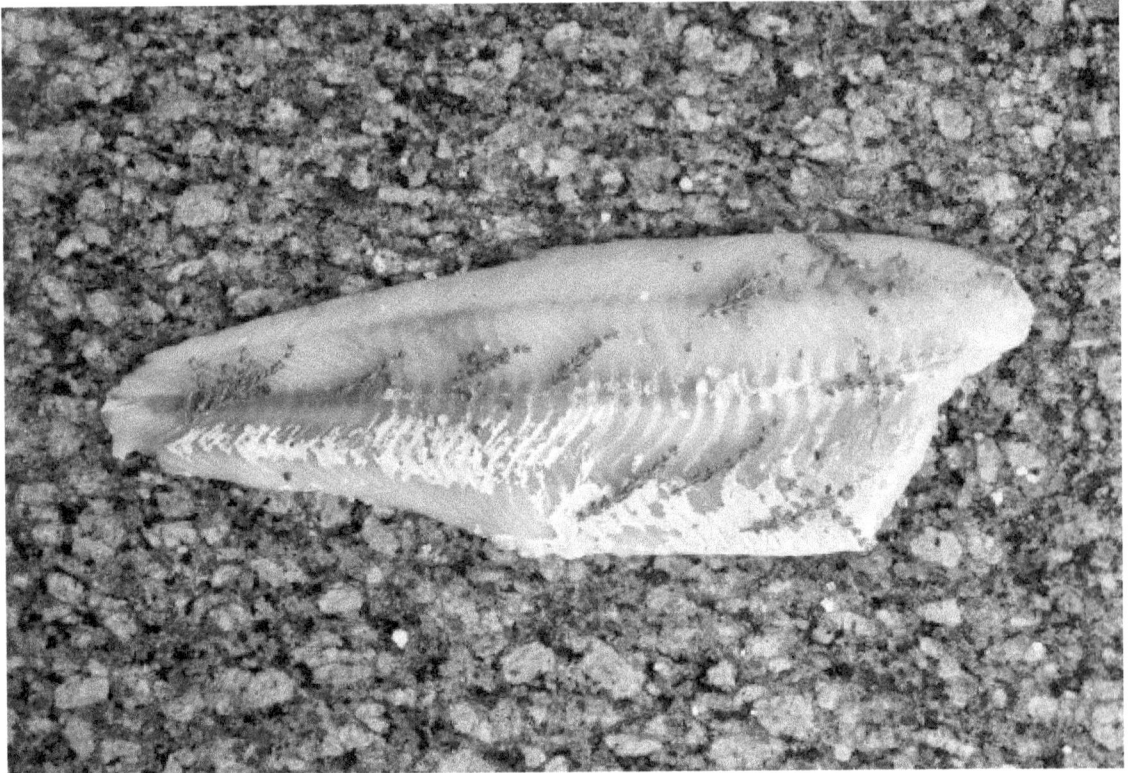

Barramundi is fish native to the Australia coastline; this recipe combines any Aussie beer to create a delicious family snack time.

Preparation Time: 65 minutes

Yield: 6

Ingredient List:

- 24 barramundi strips
- 1 cup tempura flour
- 1 chilled Aussie original dark beer
- 1 tsp fresh chili ground
- 1 tsp baking soda
- Vegetable oil for frying
- Salt and pepper

Preparation:

Mix the chili in the beer and bring to a simmer

This will make bring out the aroma

Refrigerate and then mix in the tempura flour and baking soda

Season the fish fillets, dip into the beer batter, and fry until it is brown and crisp

Serve with mayo and ketchup sauce

Spicy Grilled Figs with Vanilla Ice cream

Fig is one fruit you never know how to eat it. Well, until you are in Australia.

Preparation Time: 12 minutes

Yield: 2

Ingredient List:

- 3 figs cut in halves
- 1 tsp sweet chili sauce
- 2 tbsp brown sugar

Preparation:

Heat the grill

Mix the sugar with the sweet chili sauce

Rub the mixture on the face of the figs

Grill face down and over for 5 to 7 minutes
It should be soft and almost falling apart

Sweet and Tangy Pavlova

What is there not to love? This is a pie that has all the flavors to tickle your taste buds.

Preparation Time: 120 minutes

Yield: 6 – 8

Ingredient List:

- 1 jar lemon/lime syrup store-bought
- ¼ cup passion fruits
- 1 tbsp lime & lemon zest
- 2 tbsp lime & lemon juice
- 6 large eggs white alone
- 45ml sherry vinegar
- 1 tsp lemon essence
- 1 tsp vanilla

- 3.5 cups caster sugar
- 3 tbsp cornflour
- Pinch salt
- 60ml or ¼ cup hot water

Preparation:
First, beat the eggs on high until it starts to stiffen up
Add the sugar while whisking
Add the rest of the ingredients and water at the end (the peaks should be stiff)
Next, scoop onto a baking tray and spread into a circle
Bake until it is set and cracking
Allow it to cool and top with the syrup, passion fruit, and cream if you like

Minty Flavor Roasted Baliman Bug

Do not get grossed out yet; these are like lobsters except they are shorter, flatter and well like bugs.

Preparation Time: 15 minutes

Yield: 4

Ingredient List:

- 4 large bugs
- ½ cup butter melted
- 2 tbsp mint
- 2 tbsp basil
- 1 small shallot
- 1 small chili
- 1 tsp minced garlic

- 1 tsp cumin
- Salt and pepper

Preparation:
Blend the ingredients except for the bugs together
Clean the bugs and use a knife to divide it into two
Place on an open fire and brush the mix all over
Cook for 5 to 8 minutes, basting at intervals
Serve with the mixture

Double Chocolate Milo Pops

Milo is a classic beverage for most Aussie homes, and this recipe is for kids.

Preparation Time: 30 minutes

Yield: 12

Ingredient List:

- 4 cups rice bubbles
- 2 cups cocoa pops
- ½ cup Milo
- 2 cups milk chocolate melt

Preparation:

Melt the chocolate melt over a double boiler

Add the rest of the ingredients and mix it well

Scoop into lined muffin tins and allow it to cool

Serve

Spicy Grilled Kangaroo Meat in Tacos

These are deep dark colored meat and take very well to flavors. Cook them anyhow you want but do not overcook them.

Preparation Time: 80 minutes
Yield: 4
Ingredient List:

- 1 jar store-bought tomato salsa
- 500g fresh cut kangaroo meat
- 1 tsp black pepper
- 1 tsp ginger powder
- 1 tsp garlic powder
- 1 tsp cumin
- ½ tsp nutmeg

- 1 tsp chili flakes
- 1 tsp paprika
- Salt
- 1 tbsp olive oil

Preparation:
First, in a bowl, mix the dry ingredients together
Slice the meat into thin sheets
Apply olive oil and massage
Next, coat the meat with the spice very well
Grill until tender but still slightly pink
Then, remove from heat and cover to rest
Chop and serve in a taco

Peanut Crusted Chicken Schnitzel

Everybody loves breaded chicken, and this is absolutely divine and easy to make too,

Preparation Time: 40 minutes

Yield: 4

Ingredient List:

- 6 boneless chicken thighs beaten flat (thighs are juicier)
- 1 cup roasted ground peanut
- ½ cup coconut flour
- 1 tbsp chili flakes
- 1 tsp cloves
- 1 tsp garlic and ginger powder
- Salt and pepper
- 2 tbsp oil

- Oil for frying

Preparation:
In a bowl, mix the ingredients except for the chicken and oil
Rub the chicken with oil and coat with the mix
Pat down and shake off any excess
Fry in oil until brown

Aussie Pine Cap Burger Patties

Australians love burgers. Whether it is going out or making one at home, there is always a burger at the end of the tunnel.

Preparation Time: 30 minutes

Yield: 4

Ingredient List:

- 200g fresh round pine cap mushroom
- 300g ground beef
- 2 tbsp bacon fat
- 1 small onion chopped
- 1 tsp garlic and ginger minced each
- 1 large egg
- Salt and pepper

- 1 tbsp pineapple puree

Preparation:
First, squeeze any excess water from the mushrooms and pat it down with a kitchen towel
Add the mushroom in a bowl with the beef, fat, onion, ginger, and garlic
Next, stir to combine, add the egg, pineapple puree, and season to taste
Mix well and make into patties
Keep in a refrigerator to chill for 10 minutes to enable the flavor to marry
Lastly, grill or cook in a cast iron pan

Aussie Spicy Apricot Chicken

Australia grows a lot of fruits, and apricots are one of them. This delicious fruit pairs with some heat to create the best chicken recipe you will ever eat.

Preparation Time: 180 minutes

Yield: 6

Ingredient List:

- 8 skin-on, bone-in chicken thighs
- 4 fresh apricots chopped
- 1 tbsp apricot preserved
- 2 cups chicken stock
- 1 tbsp freshly grated ginger
- 1 tsp chopped red chili
- 1 tsp crushed black pepper

- 2 tbsp oyster sauce
- 2 tbsp coriander leaves chopped
- Salt and pepper to taste
- 3 tbsp vegetable oil

Preparation:
Season the chicken and brown with the oil in a slow cooker
Add the remaining ingredients into it and cover to cook
The chicken should be fall off the bone tender
Serve with jasmine rice

A little Mediterranean Twist on the Aussie Scone

Scones are the easiest way to a hearty breakfast. You can stick to the original ancestral recipe, but a twist is welcome.

Preparation Time: 30 minutes

Yield: 6

Ingredient List:

- 3 cups self-raising flour – double sifted
- 1 cup Medjool dates
- 1 large egg
- 2 tbsp shortening
- 1 tbsp Greek yogurt
- 2 tbsp sugar
- ½ tsp black pepper

- Salt to taste
- 1 tbsp melted butter

Preparation:
Beat the eggs shortening, yogurt, sugar, salt, and black pepper in a mixer
Add the flour. Then, fold in the date
Gather together on a board and gently bring the dough in a single manner
Place on a baking tray and cook for ten minutes
Remove from the oven and brush with a brush
Return to the oven for another 10 minutes
Serve warm or cold

Cinnamon-Chili Rub Pan-Fried Lamb Pops

Lamb is a very subtle piece of meat that takes to flavors, and this dish is incredible. You do need to do some work scrapping down the bone to look good.

Preparation Time: 50 minutes

Yield: 4

Ingredient List:

- 8 2-cm thick lamb chops
- 1 tsp garlic paste
- 1 tsp salt
- 1 tsp black pepper
- 1 tsp chopped rosemary
- 1 tsp chili flakes
- 1 tsp cinnamon powder

- 2 tbsp butter

Preparation:
Use a carving knife to scrape down the bony parts to be neat
Mix the rest of the ingredients together in a bowl
Apply generously over the lamb and let it sit for 15 minutes
Heat a large non-stick pan and brown on all sides for 2 minutes
Place pan in the oven to finish off
Serve with garlic herb butter

Savory Impossible Pie

Guess Aussies wondered how you could make a pie without a base, welcome a quiche or impossible pie.

Preparation Time: 50 minutes

Yield: 6

Ingredient List:

- ½ cup diced onion
- 1 cup diced ham
- 1 red & green bell pepper diced
- ½ cup coconut flour
- 4 large eggs, lightly beaten
- ½ cup cheddar cheese
- ½ cup Swiss cheese, grated
- 1 cup smoked shrimps diced

- 300ml milk
- 1 tsp garlic powder
- Salt & black pepper
- 1 tbsp butter

Preparation:
Fry and caramelize the with the diced peppers
Spread the onion mix at the base of the ramekin
Scatter the shrimps, ham, and cheeses in any order
Mix the flour eggs with the milk and garlic powder
Pour through a strain into the pan to remove any lumps
Place the mixture in an oven to cook until its set and crusty brown on top
Serve

Chocolate and Nuts Cookies

Australia is home to lots of cookies. And these are getting a little healthier with macadamia in them.

Preparation Time: 25 minutes

Yield: a lot

Ingredient List:

- 1 packet store-bought cookie dough
- 1 cup toasted coconut flakes
- ½ cup toasted macadamia nuts
- 1 cup dark chocolate chips

Preparation:
Gently roll out the dough
Sprinkle the coconut flakes all over

Fold and roll out again
Cut to size
Insert the chocolate chips and macadamia nuts in each cookie
Bake on a parchment-lined tray
Remove when the edges are golden and brown
Enjoy

Good Old Cornish Handheld Pastry

Food for miners has now become a classic dish for everyone. This pie is hearty and rich and filled to the brim with flavor.

Preparation Time: 60 minutes

Yield: 8

Ingredient List:

- 600g half pork/beef ground combo – pork adds a depth of richness
- 1 cup chopped white onions
- 2 large carrots diced
- 2 cups diced potatoes
- ¼ cup beef stock
- 1 tsp minced garlic
- 1 tsp chili deseeded

- 2 tbsp chicken fat
- 2 tbsp milk liquid
- 1kg store-bought puff pastry

Preparation:
Add the chicken fat to a pan, sauté the onions until soft
Next, add the ground meat and cook until brown
Add the potatoes, carrot, garlic, minced garlic, chili, and season well
Add the stock and cook until mushy but still separate
Next, dust the board with flour and roll out the pastry
Cut and fill with the cool
Fold and seal with a fork
Then, place on a baking tray. Bush with milk
Bake for 15 to 20 minutes

Beef Shashliks with Veggie on a stick

Just like a kebab, better than a kebab, and it is so easy to make too.

Preparation Time: 65 minutes

Yield: 4

Ingredient List:

- 24 rounds sweet potatoes
- 2kg beef tenderloin cut in chunks
- 2 tbsp Outback steakhouse steak seasoning
- 1 tbsp fresh rosemary chopped
- 5 apricots cored and cut into large cubes
- 1 large onion cut into chunks
- 1 tsp small chili chopped
- ¼ cup olive oil

- 1 tsp minced garlic
- Salt and black pepper

Preparation:
In a bowl, add all the ingredients. Then, allow it to sit overnight for maximum flavor
In the morning, heat the coal
Using a wet skewer, insert beef, potato, apricot, meat, onion, and meat
Repeat until done
Place on the grill and use the marinade to baste the beef until done
Serve with yogurt sauce

Minty, Spicy Lamb Pie

Some refreshing flavors after a kick of pepper, this pie is simple and delicious and a great crowd-pleaser.

Preparation Time: 120 minutes

Yield: 8-10

Ingredient List:

- 600g lamb shoulder, diced into small pieces
- ¾ cup almond flour
- ¼ cup vegetable oil or margarine
- 1 cup brown onion diced
- 2 cloves garlic
- ½ cup celery diced
- 1 cup rice wine
- 240ml beef or vegetable stock

- ½ tsp cumin seed
- 1 sheet shortcrust pastry store-bought
- 2 tbsp mint leaves chopped
- 1 sheet puff pastry store-bought
- Salt and pepper
- 1 egg yolk nicely mixed with 1 tbsp milk for brushing the dough

Preparation:
Season the meat, toss in the flour, and fry until brown and almost crisp
Remove and add the cumin seed to release its aroma
Add the onion, garlic, and celery until soft
Add the lamb, wine, stock, and allow it to cook until lamb is tender in a thick sauce
Roll the shortcrust pastry on a floured board, and cut into the desired shape
Fill it will the filling and cover with the puff pastry sheets
Brush with the egg mix and bake until brown, about 15 to 25 minutes

Pan-Fried Prawns with Chili Lime Cilantro Butter

These are delicious, especially if you can get fresh prawns from the fishermen at the docks.

Preparation Time: 30 minutes

Yield: 4

Ingredient List:

- 2 tbsp cilantro chopped
- 1 tsp garlic chopped
- ¼ cup butter
- 1 small red chili diced
- 1 tsp lime zest
- ½ tsp lime juice
- Salt and black pepper to taste
- 2 dozen fresh, cleaned, and deveined prawns

- ½ tbsp oil

Preparation:
Season the prawns with salt and pepper
Add the oil to the pan and cook them
When they start to turn pink
Add the rest of the ingredients except the lime juice
Cook for 5 to 7 minutes
Remove and place in a bowl
Add the lime juice to deglaze the pan
Stir for 30 seconds and pour over the prawns
Serve

Oven Fried Lemongrass Fish Wedges

Australia is surrounded by water, which gives room for a variety of seafood recipes. This one is for picky kids.

Preparation Time: 45 minutes

Yield: 8

Ingredient List:

- 1 tbsp finely chopped dill
- ½ cup grated parmesan
- ½ cup crushed cornflakes
- 1 tsp garlic, onion, ginger powder each
- 1 tsp chili flakes
- 1 egg beaten
- 8 white fish rectangles

- ½ cup olive oil
- Salt and pepper

Preparation:s
Add the olive oil to a baking tray and preheat the oven
In a bowl, mix the first four ingredients together
In another bowl, beat the eggs and chili together with a little salt
Season the fish steaks, dip in egg, and press the dry coating around it
Arrange the fish in the heated tray and cook
Turing at intervals until brown and crisp

Madura Green Tea Bag Fruit Loaf

This is Australia in all its glory. The delicious, light and melt in your mouth loaf complete your afternoon tea time.

Preparation Time: 65 minutes

Yield: 12

Ingredient List:

- 2 Madura green tea bags boiled in 300ml water
- 200g mixed dried fruits
- 50g coconut bits
- 50g toasted almonds
- 2 cups cake flour
- 1/3 cup almond flour
- ¾ cup brown sugar

- 1 tsp cinnamon

Preparation:
Drain the tea, add the mixed dried fruits, cinnamon, and sugar; refrigerate overnight or for 6 hours
In the morning, whisk in the eggs, flour, almond, and coconut bits
Line a loaf tin with parchment paper. Then, let it come above the edges
Pour into the tin. Bake until a skewer comes out clean

Grilled Peaches and Feta Salad

This is a classic Aussie ingredient that can be used in all manners – Peaches.

Preparation Time: 10 minutes

Yield: 2

Ingredient List:

- 3 large juicy peaches seed removed and cut into wedges
- Crumbled feta cheese
- 1 tsp oil
- 300g rocket leaves
- ¼ cup roasted pecans
- ¼ cup slices of sweet white onion thinly sliced

Preparation:

Drizzle some oil on the peaches and grill for 2 minutes
Add the rockets and onions to a bowl with the grilled peaches
Crumble the feta on it, and add the pecans

Rich Caramel Filled Anzac Muffins

Start your morning healthy and delicious with these Aussie muffins; they can be made the night before.

Preparation Time: 30 minutes

Yield: 12

Ingredient List:

- 12 toffees
- 1.24 cups buttermilk
- 120g unsalted butter soften
- ¼ cup light corn syrup
- 1.75 cups APF
- 1 tbsp rolled oats
- 1/3 cup white sugar
- 1/3 cup dark brown sugar

- 150g toasted coconut flakes
  - 1 large egg
  - Extra brown sugar and oats as toppings

Preparation:
Bring the buttermilk, butter, and corn syrup to a gentle simmer and set aside
Combine the dry ingredients in a bowl – flour, oats, sugar, and coconut flakes
When the milk mixture is cold, whisk in the egg
Pour the wet mixture into the dry ingredients and fold
Scoop the batter into sprayed muffin tins
Add a toffee inside each muffin and sprinkle with oats and sugar
Bake until a skewer comes out clean
Serve

Vegemite Beef Roll

There is no Australian home that does not have a jar of vegemite in their pantry. This salty, bitter and yeasty sauce adds the 6th flavor to food – umami.

Preparation Time: 45 minutes

Yield: 6

Ingredient List:

- 500g pure beef diced into tiny bits
- 2 cups onions diced
- ½ cup diced carrots
- 1 cup parmesan
- ¼ cup vegemite
- 2 tbsp cornstarch slurry
- Salt & black pepper
- ¼ cup stock or water

- ¼ cup oil
- 1 sheet puff pastry
- 1 egg beaten

Preparation:
Add the oil to a pan and cook the beef until cooked
Add the onion and carrots with salt and black pepper
Cook with ¼ cup of water or stock for 5 to 7 minutes
Add the slurry and vegemite to thicken
Allow it to cool, then stir in the parmesan
Roll out the puff pastry
Spread the filling on one side and roll
Cut into squares and brush with the egg
Bake until brown and golden

It is a Tim Tam Cheesecake

Tim Tam is a classic Australian biscuit. It does add a malty flavor to this cheesecake.

Preparation Time: 50 minutes

Yield: 4

Ingredient List:

- 3 packets Tim Tam biscuits
- ¼ cup melted butter
- 2 tbsp Milo
- 500g cream cheese at room temperature
- 4 tbsp caster sugar
- 360g melted white chocolate
- 1.5 cups heavy cream
- 200g melted milk chocolate

Preparation:

Line a 6-inch pan and set aside

Blend a packet of Tim Tam with butter and press down in the pan, then chill

Beat the cream cheese, sugar with the milk chocolate until fluffy

Whip the heavy cream separately and fold into the cream cheese mix

Divide the mixture and add the milk chocolate to one bowl

Line the edges with the remaining Tim Tam biscuits

Spoon the mixture into the pan, alternating it

Refrigerate overnight, and using the parchment paper to lift out of the pan

Sprinkle the Milo and cut to serve

Lord Lamington's Lamingtons

These are all the flavors you dream about in a piece of cake. It is a messy affair but overall delicious.

Preparation Time: 40 minutes

Yield: 12

Ingredient List:

- 1 box vanilla cake mix
- 2 tbsp butter
- ½ cup milk
- 2 tbsp good cocoa powder
- 400g icing sugar
- 2 cups sweetened coconut flakes

Preparation:

First, follow the own instructions on the cake mix pack to mix accurately
Pour the batter into an 8-inch pan and place to bake
Meanwhile, bring to a boil the milk and butter in a pan
Next, remove from heat and sieve in the icing sugar and cocoa powder
It should be thick but pourable
Gradually remove the cake and cool on a rack
Next, when it is completely cool, pour the icing all over
Sprinkle the coconut flakes covering all corners
Chill, cut, and serve

As Easy As a Damper Loaf

This roughly shaped Aussie loaf is a classic that pairs well with all types of spreads. You do not have to have any special baking skills to knock one out of the park.

Preparation Time: 50 minutes

Yield: 6

Ingredient List:

- 500g bread flour
- 1 tsp baking powder
- 1 cup full-fat milk
- 1 large
- 1 tbsp sugar
- 1 tsp melted butter

Preparation:
Add the egg, sugar, and milk into a mixer
Gradually add the flour until a dough is formed
Scoop the dough out and knead until smooth
Roughly shape as desire and brush with butter
Bake until a hollow sound is heard when tapped
Serve

Aussie Classic Chiko Rolls

These are like spring rolls but are an Australian classic sold in stores in the country. Today you can replicate yours and enjoy unique flavors worth the effort.

Preparation Time: 40 minutes

Yield: 6

Ingredient List:

- Oil for frying
- Large spring roll wrapper
- 1 large onion julienned
- 2 large carrots julienned
- 1 celery stalk julienned
- 1 green and red pepper julienned
- 1 small chili diced in bits

- 1 small-sized cabbage head julienned
- 1 tbsp oil
- 1 tsp garlic
- ½ tsp ginger
- Salt and white pepper

Preparation:
Add the oil to the pan and sauté the onion, garlic, ginger, and chili
Add the cabbage, carrots, celery and cook down until the soft and the liquid evaporated – you do not want a soggy roll
Add the filling, fold the edges, and roll using water as glue
Deep fry. Then, serve with sweet chili sauce

Fresh and Down To Earth Salad

This salad combines the tartness of plum, the earthiness of beet, and the sweet ricotta in honey, and it is delicious.

Preparation Time: 20 minutes

Yield: 2

Ingredient List:

- 6 plums cored and cut in wedges
- 3 small baby beets thinly sliced
- ¼ cup creamy ricotta
- 1 tbsp honey
- 1 tbsp olive oil
- 1 tbsp red wine vinegar
- Salt and black pepper

Preparation:
Gently grill the plums to release their juices
Next, add them to a bowl with the beets
Mix the honey, oil, vinegar in a bowl
Add a scoop of ricotta cheese
Next, sprinkle with salt and pepper
Drizzle over the dressing
Serve

Sweet Mango and Chili Fried Prawns

Sweet, sour, spicy, all flavors play a role in bringing the robust flavor to this dish. All you need is fresh ingredient to get it right.

Preparation Time: 30 minutes

Yield: 4

Ingredient List:

- 1 cup mango stripes
- Handful roasted cashew
- 2 tbsp cilantro chopped
- 12 jumbo prawns cleaned and deveined
- 1 tbsp full butter
- 1 clove minced garlic
- 2 tbsp sweet chili sauce

- 1 tsp chili finely chopped
- ¼ cup rice wine
- Salt to taste

Preparation:
Add the butter to the pan and sauté the chili and garlic
Add the prawns and cook until pink
Add the sweet chili sauce, rice wine, and cashew nuts
Cover to cook for 2 minutes
Add the mango and cilantro
Stir and serve

Conclusion

Australia may be called the country down under, but it is filled with beautiful flavors that will make you palette dance with joy. It does not matter how you cook it; the natural taste will always shine through. If you are visiting Australia, remember to enjoy some local drinks too.

[]

Don't miss out!

Visit the website below and you can sign up to receive emails whenever Ida Smith publishes a new book. There's no charge and no obligation.

https://books2read.com/r/B-A-LRXL-FWVJB

BOOKS 2 READ

Connecting independent readers to independent writers.